I Thought I'd Take My Rat to School

Poems for September to June

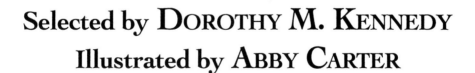

Selected by DOROTHY M. KENNEDY
Illustrated by ABBY CARTER

Little, Brown and Company
Boston   New York   Toronto   London

First Edition

Copyright acknowledgments appear on page 62.

Library of Congress Cataloging-in-Publication Data

I thought I'd take my rat to school : poems for September to June /
selected by Dorothy M. Kennedy ; illustrated by Abby Carter. — 1st
ed.
    p.   cm.
    Summary: A collection of poems capturing the good and the bad
sides of school, by such authors as Russell Hoban, Gary Soto, and
Karla Kuskin.
    ISBN 0-316-48893-3
    1. Education — Juvenile poetry.   2. Children's poetry, American.
3. Schools — Juvenile poetry.   [1. Schools — Poetry.   2. American
poetry — Collections.]   I. Kennedy, Dorothy M. (Dorothy Mintzlaff)
II. Carter, Abby, ill.
PS595.E38I17   1993
811'.50809282 — dc20   92-12775

10   9   8   7   6   5   4   3   2   1

BP

Published simultaneously in Canada
by Little, Brown & Company (Canada) Limited

Printed in the United States of America

For my family, with love
— D. M. K.

For Samantha
— A. C.

Contents

School Buses

You'd think that by the end of June they'd take themselves
Away, get out of sight — but no, they don't; they
Don't at all. You see them waiting through
July in clumps of sumac near the railroad, or
Behind a service station, watching, always watching for a
Child who's let go of summer's hand and strayed. I have
Seen them hunting on the roads of August — empty buses
Scanning woods and ponds with rows of empty eyes. This morning
I saw five of them, parked like a week of
Schooldays, smiling slow in orange paint and
Smirking with their mirrors in the sun —
But summer isn't done! Not yet!

Russell Hoban

Back to School

When summer smells like apples
and shadows feel cool
and falling leaves make dapples
of color on the pool
and wind is in the maples
and sweaters are the rule
and hazy days spell lazy ways,
it's hard to go to school.

But I go!

Aileen Fisher

September   Bini'ant'aatsoh*

Alice pulls her hair back into one long braid.
Last year's gym shorts are too short. She's grown.
Her toes won't even wiggle
in last year's tennies.
It's a mile through the dust
to the yellow bus stop. In winter: through mud.
The pup seems to beg with his eyes:
"Stay home. Let's us play, Alice Yazzie.
The two of us."

Grandfather frowns.
"We do what we must.
I see you must go to school. This year —
not so many hot dogs in the cafeteria.
More books in the learning center.
We'll see to that."
Grandfather sits on the school board
and helps decide about classes and buildings.
The oldest school board man, he sees change happening.
He says it must come.
He even voted for girls to play football
if they want to. And study mechanical drawing.

* Navajo word for September

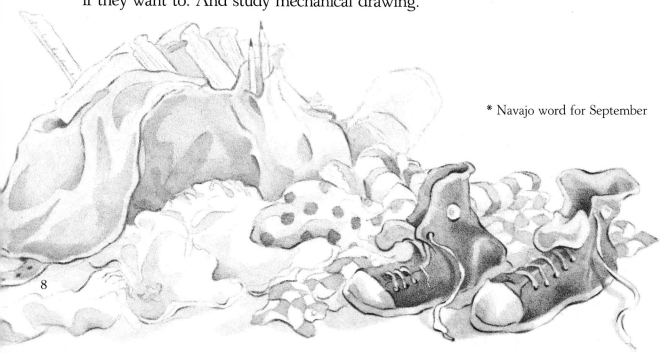

8

Alice starts off in her tie-dyed T-shirt
and a denim skirt faded canyon blue.
Grandfather calls. He gives Alice a ride
behind him, on his horse,
to the bus stop shelter.
Alice is surprised.
"Remember," says Grandfather,
nudging the old mare until she faces around.
"You don't have to take mechanical drawing
if you don't want to."

"Thank you, Grandfather."
As they move off, old man on old horse,
Alice feels winter coming.

Ramona Maher

Going to School

From here to there
or anywhere
is longer in the morning.
It doesn't seem so far by blocks
but first I have to find some socks
that match.
I have to brush this
and tie those
and tuck that.
There's a clock on the wall
ticking, "Hurry don't fall,"
as I run down the hall.
Well, I won't fall at all.

Out the door
down the block.
"Good morning tree,
hello there rock,"
(In my head the ticking clock).
I'm running
I'm walking
I watch a cat stalking a bird
through the bushes
but I'm on my way.
I know I'm not yet there
I never may get there
with small stones for kicking
and weeds for picking.
That dog down the block
lobs a bark at the day.

My math's in my pocket,
my pencil is here
in my hair where I put it
in back of my ear.
I tripped and I dropped it.
It dropped and I kicked it.
I kicked it and stopped it.
It's near
where?
There
here.

I get to the corner.
I stop at the corner.
The light at the corner
goes green with a wink.
The bell begins ringing
and I begin running.
I run
and it's ringing.
I made it . . .
I think.

Karla Kuskin

Going to School

Going to school
I pass a street
where there is a hardware store
and next to it
a flower shop.
I like to stop
and greet
the flowers on display,
then see next door
different kinds of blooms:
bright paint cans,
shiny pots and pans,
a bouquet
of mops and brooms.

Eve Merriam

Weathermen, Weathermen

Weathermen, weathermen
Have only one rule:
They make it rain
When there is no school.

Louis Phillips

I Thought I'd Take My Rat to School

I thought I'd take my rat to school
   To show my nice new teacher.
     "Aaaeeeiiiiiiieeaa!" she said.
   "Get out, you horrid creature!"

Colin McNaughton

The pig has a pen

The pig has a pen
The bear has a den
The trout has a pool
While I have school

The crow has a nest
The hawk has a quest
The owl has a mate
Doggone! I'm late!

David McCord

Cruel Boys

First day. Jackie and I walking in leaves
On our way to becoming 8th graders,
Pencils behind our ears, pee-chee folders
Already scribbled with football players
In dresses, track star in a drooped bra.
We're tough. I'm Mexican
And he's an unkillable Okie with three
Teeth in his pocket, sludge under
His nails from scratching oily pants.
No one's going to break us, not the dean
Or principal, not the cops
Who could arrive in pairs, walkie-talkies
To their mouths, warning:
"Dangerous. They have footballs."
We could bounce them off their heads
And reporters might show up
With shirt sleeves rolled up to their ears,
Asking our age, if we're Catholic.
But this never happens. We go to first
Period, math, then second period, geography,
And in third period, English, the woman
Teacher reads us Frost, something
About a tree, and to set things straight,
How each day will fall like a tree.
Jackie raises his hand, stands up,
And shouts, "You ain't nothing but a hound dog,"
As the spitballs begin to fly.

Gary Soto

Remembering:
The First Day of School

"Write a composition,"
said the teacher,
"about something you did
during summer vacation.
Make it two pages long
and neatness counts."

I sat there
remembering the quiet
of the giant redwoods.
Even my little brother
whispered.

"Teacher,
could I write a poem
instead?"

Bobbi Katz

15

The New Boy

The door swung inward. I stood and breathed
The new-school atmosphere:
The smell of polish and disinfectant,
And the flavor of my own fear.

I followed into the cloakroom; the walls
Rang to the shattering noise
Of boys who barged and boys who banged;
Boys and still more boys!

A boot flew by me. Its angry owner
Pursued with force and yell;
Somewhere a man snapped orders; somewhere
There clanged a warning bell.

And there I hung with my new schoolmates;
They pushing and shoving me; I
Unknown, unwanted, pinned to the wall;
On the verge of ready-to-cry.

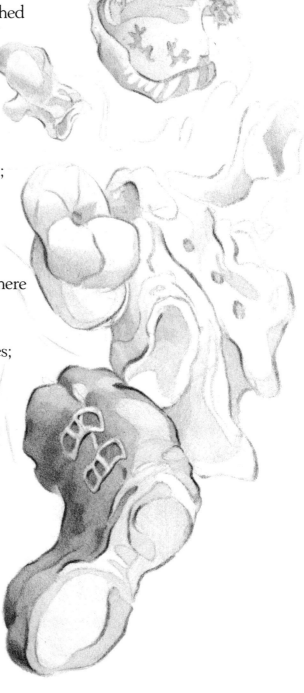

Then, from the doorway, a boy called out:
"Hey, you over there! You're new!
Don't just stand there propping the wall up!
I'll look after you!"

I turned; I timidly raised my eyes;
He stood and grinned meanwhile;
And my fear died, and my lips answered
Smile for his smile.

He showed me the basins, the rows of pegs;
He hung my cap at the end;
He led me away to my new classroom . . .
And now that boy's my friend.

John Walsh

Barrio School

We start school late this year
because the bean crop was late, so we are late to go
to the brick school to pick the numbers off the vines
carefully, so the fractions won't snap.

We study wars
I didn't know about & bearded Abe
who didn't free anybody I know. I like the gym
with floorwax you can skate on, I like lunch —
tortillas from home, red grapes & chocolate milk
like sweet brown mud — I like the globe
that spins on poles, & poetry,
& the parakeet in its cage, & half-past-two
that frees Susana my best friend & me.

We link arms, skip downstreet
happy as 2 fleas,
jumping old flat-out dogs
& napping fire hydrants.

Julia Flores-Morales

18

education

mama got out and fussed
real good 'bout the schools
cause i'm in the eighth
grade and she wants me to continue
but she says she needs to be
sure i don't become
just another high
school student

Nikki Giovanni

I don't understand

I don't understand
how "good" English
and five times two is ten
can help buy us more food
and extra blankets.
But Mama says it can
and she never lied to me.
So I ask my teachers,
but they don't tell.
I bet they know.
Why won't they say?

Nikki Grimes

Teacher

My teacher looked at me and frowned
A look that must have weighed a pound

And said: When I was young as you
There were some things I did not do.

X. J. Kennedy

Duty of the Student

It is the duty of the student
Without exception to be prudent.
If smarter than his teacher, tact
Demands that he conceal the fact.

Edward Anthony

No Place for a Snack

You're not allowed to eat in class
Or even nibble at your thumb —
No candy bar,
No raisin cake,
No cookie, carrot,
Peach, or plum.

Though coughdrops may be sucked, we hear,
You may not suck a pickle, dear,
(But if you DO, to be polite,
Give Mr. Jones a little bite).

Norah Smaridge

Those Who Do Not Study History Are Doomed

It is so hard   to read   about   the glories
of growing cotton in   the   ante   bellum
South, when my Northern teeth sit idle in
my   c o n t e m p o r a r y   empty   mouth.

The   past   was   last   night's   double   fudge
d e l i g h t
and I can almost taste the p r e s e n t
as my chocolate bar melts under a   fading
S o u t h e r n   s u n.

Arnold Adoff

Arithmetic

Multiplication is vexation,
Division is as bad;
The Rule of Three it puzzles me,
And fractions drive me mad.

Anonymous

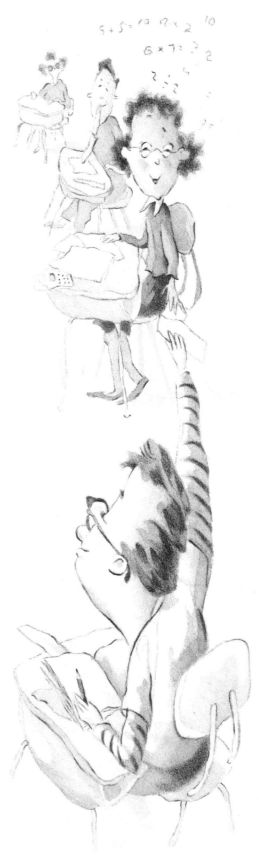

Equations

Pi r squared is forty-two,
Diameter is three,
Two and two add up to four,
(Do you love me?)
X and Y equations,
Add the number two,
Twelve and twelve are twenty-four,
(I love you.)

Patricia Hubbell

Math Class

She talks about the decimal point,
The reasons why —
But on the window, buzzing free,
A fly

With two red eyes
Moves slowly up the pane.
She moves the decimal one place left
And then again

The fly moves up
And up, practiced and slow.
What I have learned of decimal points
Flies know.

Myra Cohn Livingston

$5 + 5 = 10 \qquad 10 + 10 = 20 \qquad 20 + 20 = 90$

Arithmetic

Arithmetic is where numbers fly like pigeons in and out of your head.
Arithmetic tells you how many you lose or win if you know how many you
      had before you lost or won.
Arithmetic is seven eleven all good children go to heaven — or five six
      bundle of sticks.
Arithmetic is numbers you squeeze from your head to your hand to your
      pencil to your paper till you get the answer.
Arithmetic is where the answer is right and everything is nice and you can
      look out of the window and see the blue sky — or the answer is wrong
      and you have to start all over and try again and see how it comes out
      this time.
If you take a number and double it and double it again and then double
      it a few more times, the number gets bigger and bigger and goes
      higher and higher and only arithmetic can tell you what the number
      is when you decide to quit doubling.
Arithmetic is where you have to multiply — and you carry the multiplication
      table in your head and hope you won't lose it.
If you have two animal crackers, one good and one bad, and you eat one
      and a striped zebra with streaks all over him eats the other, how many
      animal crackers will you have if somebody offers you five six seven
      and you say No no no and you say Nay nay nay and you say Nix
      nix nix?
If you ask your mother for one fried egg for breakfast and she gives you
      two fried eggs and you eat both of them, who is better in arithmetic,
      you or your mother?

Carl Sandburg

Propper English

Once upon a time I used
To mispell
To sometimes split infinitives
To get words of out order
To punctuate, badly
To confused my tenses
to ignore capitals
To employ "common or garden" clichés
To exaggerate hundreds of times a day
But worst of all I used
To forget to finish what I

Alan F. G. Lewis

Difference

On paper that's ruled
or plain and white,
with pencil in hand
we sit and write.

On meadows of snow
spread white and neat,
little *mice* write
with tails and feet.

Aileen Fisher

Egyptian Hieroglyphic Writing

On tombs and walls
And jewels and cliffs
Egyptians carved their
Hieroglyphs.
A picture writing
Cut in stone,
In amber, ivory,
Bronze and bone.

If they chiseled
The wrong place
I wonder how
They could erase?

Mary O'Neill

The Eraser Poem

The eraser poem.
The eraser poem
The eraser poe
The eraser po
The eraser p
The eraser
The erase
The eras
The era
The er
The e
The
Th
T
-

Louis Phillips

Recess

The children
scribble their shadows
on the school yard,

scribble
scribble
on a great blackboard —

lanky leg
shadows
running into
lifted arm shadows
flinging
bouncing ball shapes
into skinny upside down shadows
swinging
on
long monkey bars

till
a cloud
moving
across the morning sun
wipes out all
scribbles
like a giant
eraser.

Lilian Moore

In the Playground

In the playground
Some run round
Chasing a ball
Or chasing each other;
Some pretend to be
Someone on TV;
Some walk
And talk,
Some stand
On their hands
Against the wall
And some do nothing at all.

Stanley Cook

Catching

The boys catch the girls
And the girls catch the boys:
Kissing in the schoolyard,
What a yucky noise!

Dennis Lee

The Gerbil

The gerbil stands up
Crouching like a kangaroo
Ready to hop;
To him the children he sees
Seem tall as trees;
His paws clutch
The teacher's hand
That stretches like a branch
Above the sand
Of the tiny desert
In his hutch.

Stanley Cook

The Creature in the Classroom

It appeared inside our classroom
at a quarter after ten,
it gobbled up the blackboard,
three erasers and a pen.
It gobbled teacher's apple
and it bopped her with the core.
"How dare you!" she responded.
"You must leave us . . . there's the door."

The creature didn't listen
but described an arabesque
as it gobbled all her pencils,
seven notebooks and her desk.
Teacher stated very calmly,
"Sir! You simply cannot stay.
I'll report you to the principal
unless you go away!"

But the thing continued eating,
it ate paper, swallowed ink.
As it gobbled up our homework,
I believe I saw it wink.
Teacher finally lost her temper.
"OUT!" she shouted at the creature.
The creature hopped beside her
and GLOPP . . . it gobbled teacher.

Jack Prelutsky

History

And I'm thinking how to get out
Of this stuffy room
With its big blackboards.

And I'm trying not to listen
In this boring room
To the way things *were*.

And I'm thinking about later,
Running from the room
Back into the world,

And what the guys will say when
I'm up to bat and hit
A big fat home run.

Myra Cohn Livingston

34

Science Lesson

In their pond, a big old baking
    Pan, our wiggly pollywogs
At their swimming lessons, shaking
    Tails, try hard to look like frogs.

During science when the teacher's
    Back is turned, mischievous Myrt
Slips six of the slippery creatures
    Down Will Weston's undershirt.

YOW! yells Will. He hits the ceiling,
    Leapfrogs Teacher's desk, and roars
Like a lion, rock-and-rolling
    Round the classroom on all fours,

Like a jumping-jack keeps hopping
    Up and down amazing fast
Till, down through his pants-legs dropping,
    Squirmy things emerge at last.

"Kids," cries Teacher, "let's start writing
    In our observation logs —
While those pollywogs were sliding
    Down Will, they've all turned to frogs!"

X. J. Kennedy

In This Last Class Before Lunch, I Close My Eyes

and think I feel the   unreal yet palpable crunch
of a chocolate-covered   fancy-foiled
decidedly   uncafeterial confection
between   my   masticating   molars.
I can taste   the sweet

                   choco late,

          warm

as it melts
against the palate of my up p er

               m o u t h

to coat and slide right down   my

              t h r o a t.

I bring a real hunger   for learning
to this last class   before lunch. I close my eyes.

Arnold Adoff

Lunch

For Plate Lunch today, I have six different choices,
Six different choices for lunches today:

The menu says Hamburger Steak with brown gravy,
    peas on the side and a pineapple slice.
The menu says Chili con Carne with crackers —
    I've already had it for lunch this week — twice!
The menu says Meatloaf — it, too, has brown gravy,
    beets on the side and a salad of slaw.
The menu says Fish Sticks with tartar sauce topping,
    and shoestring potatoes — they taste just like straw.
The menu says Tacos — right here, it says Tacos,
    but you'd never know from their shape or their size.
And finally the menu, way down at the bottom,
    says Green Noodles smothered with Chicken Surprise!

How can I choose with such choices to choose from?
Which of these lunches should I have today?

Katy Hall

The kids in my class

The kids
in my class
were laughing
and talking
and throwing
paper planes
across the room
while the teacher
was writing the test
on the blackboard.

Then everything
was quiet
and all
I could hear
was the sound
of the little kids
playing
in the schoolyard.

Eleanor Schick

Spelling Bee

It takes a good speller
to spell *cellar,*
separate, and *benefiting;*
not omitting
cemetery, cataclysm,
picnicker and *pessimism.*
And have you ever tried
innocuous, inoculate,
dessert, deserted, desiccate;
divide and *spied,*
gnat, knickers, gnome,
crumb, crypt, and *chrome;*
surreptitious, supersede,
delete, dilate, impede?

David McCord

Mixed-Up School

We have a crazy mixed-up school.
Our teacher Mrs. Cheetah
Makes us talk backwards. Nicer cat
You wouldn't want to meet a.

To start the day we eat our lunch,
Then do some heavy dome-work.
The boys' and girls' rooms go to us,
The hamster marks our homework.

At recess time we race inside
To put on diving goggles,
Play pin-the-donkey-on-the-tail,
Ball-foot or ap-for-bobbles.

Old Cheetah, with a chunk of chalk,
Writes right across two blackbirds,
And when she says, "Go home!" we walk
The whole way barefoot backwards.

X. J. Kennedy

Banananananananana

I thought I'd win the spelling bee
   And get right to the top,
But I started to spell "banana,"
   And I didn't know when to stop.

William Cole

Yawning

Sometimes — I'm sorry — but sometimes,
Sometimes, yes, sometimes I'm bored.
It may be because I'm an idiot;
It may be because I'm floored;

It may be because it is raining,
It may be because it is hot,
It may be because I have eaten
Too much, or because I have not.

But sometimes I *cannot* help yawning
(I'm sorry!) the whole morning through —
And when Teacher's turning her back on us,
It may be that she's yawning too.

Eleanor Farjeon

From the Classroom Window

Sometimes, when heads are deep in books,
And nothing stirs,
The sunlight touches that far hill,
And its three dark firs;
Then on those trees I fix my eyes —
And teacher hers.

Together awhile we contemplate
The air-blue sky
And those dark tree-tops; till, with a tiny
Start and sigh,
She turns again to the printed page —
And so do I.

But our two thoughts have met out there
Where no school is —
Where, among call of birds and faint
Shimmer of bees,
They rise in sunlight, resinous, warm —
Those dark fir-trees!

John Walsh

Puzzle

John left school.
It was sad.
There wasn't anything he had

we needed
or we even liked.
Had no skateboard. Had no bike.

He wore old shorts,
a frayed old sweater.
Guess he never had much better.

But John was cool,
a real nice guy.
Nobody knew when his mom came by

to pick him up.
He was moving away.
He never came to school next day.

He left his notebook. Left his pen.
He might come back
but who knows when?

What puzzles all of us
is why
he left, and never said good-bye.

Myra Cohn Livingston

Drawing by Ronnie C., Grade One

For the sky, blue. But the six-year-
old searching his crayon-box, finds
no blue to match that sky
framed by the window—a see-through
    shine
over treetops, housetops. The wax colors
hold only dead light, not this water-
    flash
thinning to silver
at morning's far edge.
Gray won't do, either:
gray is for rain that you make with
dark slanting lines down-paper
                            Try orange!

— Draw a large corner circle for sun,
    egg-yolk solid,
with yellow strokes, leaping outward
like fire bloom — a brightness shouting
flower-shape wind-shape joy-shape!

The boy sighs, with leg-twisting bliss
    creating . . .

It is done. The stubby crayons
(all ten of them) are stuffed back
bumpily into their box.

Ruth Lechlitner

Crayons

I've colored a picture with crayons.
   I'm not very pleased with the sun.
I'd like it much stronger and brighter
   And more like the actual one.
I've tried with the crayon that's yellow,
   I've tried with the crayon that's red.
But none of it looks like the sunlight
   I carry around in my head.

Marchette Chute

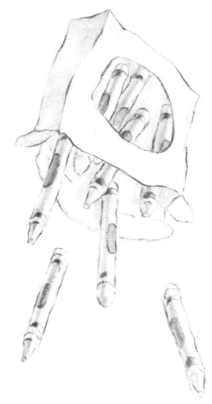

Art Class

Ms. Beecher said I don't know how
   To make a lifelike tree.
Well, all I did was look and draw
   How branches looked to me.

I *know* what you're supposed to do —
   You make a Y, and sitting
On both its arms another two
   Y's. Make them go on splitting.

I went and looked up at a bough
   With bark like scraped black leather,
And neither does a tree know how
   To fit a tree together.

X. J. Kennedy

44

Wind Circles

Without a pen,
without a hand,
without a pair of glasses,

The broken stalks
so bent and tanned
among the scattered grasses

Draw curves and circles
in the sand
with every wind that passes.

And *I*
can't draw them half as grand
in school, in drawing classes.

Aileen Fisher

What Price Glory?

I stood on a stage
And they gave me a medal
For being the
Best of the Bunch.
Then Ricky Gesumaria came by
And ate it up for lunch,
With mustard, a pickle, two slices of rye,
And a very nasty crr-rr-unch.

I stood on a stage
And they gave me a trophy
For being the
Top of the Heap.
I waited for cheers but the audience
Had fallen fast asleep,
Except for Joshua, who yelled,
"No trophies for that creep!"

I stood on a stage
And they gave me a plaque that
Said I was the
Star of the show.
It weighed a hundred pounds. Max Goldfarb
Dropped it on my toe.
And the next time someone calls my name
And wants me to stand on the stage
And get some prizes . . .
I'll still go.

Judith Viorst

School Play

I played the princess.
I had to stay
inside a barrel.
The prince hid away
in a keg right beside me.
Our hearts nearly sank
when the Pirate King said
we would both walk the plank.
Then our captain appeared
and he offered them gold
as a ransom, and that's when
the Pirate King told
us to come out
and plead our case,
and I climbed out and
slipped
and fell flat
on my face.

But it wasn't so bad
in the ending
because
all the audience gave us
a lot of
applause.

Myra Cohn Livingston

School Concert

My family was the very proudest.
They said my singing was the loudest.

Marchette Chute

Miss Norma Jean Pugh, First Grade Teacher

Full of oatmeal
And gluggy with milk
On a morning in springtime
Soft as silk
When legs feel slow
And bumblebees buzz
And your nose tickles from
Dandelion fuzz
And you long to
Break a few
Cobwebs stuck with
Diamond dew
Stretched right out
In front of you —
When all you want
To do is *feel*
Until it's time for
Another meal,
Or sit right down
In the cool
Green grass
And watch the
Caterpillars pass. . . .

Who cares if
Two and two
Are four or five
Or red or blue?
Who cares whether
Six or seven
Come before or after
Ten or eleven?
Who cares if
C-A-T
Spells cat or rat
Or tit or tat
Or ball or bat?
Well, I do
But I didn't
Used to —
Until MISS NORMA JEAN PUGH!
She's terribly old
As people go
Twenty-one-or-five-or-six
Or so
But she makes a person want to
KNOW!

Mary O'Neill

The Schoolbus Comes Before the Sun

The day drags by with textbooks
lunch cold and lumpy from a pail
an afternoon of facts
the ride by the nearer farms
where kids get off and horseplay dies
Yarrow bears the rocking of the bus
the fumes   the history teacher's growl
knows there's homework still to do
the sky already dark

Ahead   the mailbox in a drift of snow
the bus is jerking to a stop
Yarrow plunges to the road for home
to Mutt who meets him halfway there
The wiggling dog paws his shoulders
tongue warm and wet to wash away the day

Robert Currie

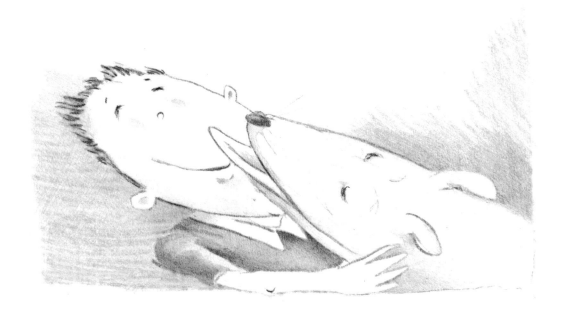

Homework

Homework sits on top of Sunday, squashing Sunday flat.
Homework has the smell of Monday, homework's very fat.
Heavy books and piles of paper, answers I don't know.
Sunday evening's almost finished, now I'm going to go
Do my homework in the kitchen. Maybe just a snack,
Then I'll sit right down and start as soon as I run back
For some chocolate sandwich cookies. Then I'll really do
All that homework in a minute. First I'll see what new
Show they've got on television in the living room.
Everybody's laughing there, but misery and gloom
And a full refrigerator are where I am at.
I'll just have another sandwich. Homework's very fat.

Russell Hoban

Homework! Oh, Homework!

Homework! Oh, homework!
I hate you! You stink!
I wish I could wash you
away in the sink,
if only a bomb
would explode you to bits.
Homework! Oh, homework!
You're giving me fits.

I'd rather take baths
with a man-eating shark,
or wrestle a lion
alone in the dark,
eat spinach and liver,
pet ten porcupines,
than tackle the homework
my teacher assigns.

Homework! Oh, homework!
You're last on my list,
I simply can't see
why you even exist,
if you just disappeared
it would tickle me pink.
Homework! Oh, homework!
I hate you! You stink!

Jack Prelutsky

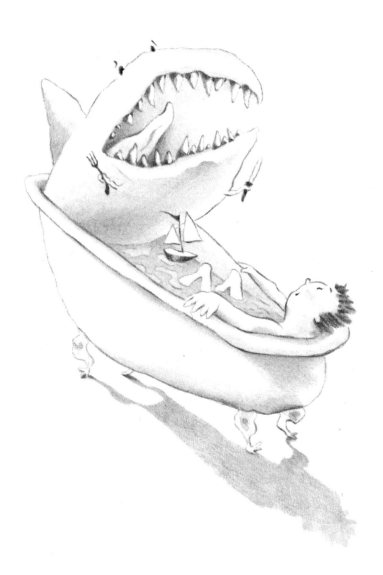

Homework

What is it about homework
That makes me want to write
My Great Aunt Myrt to thank her for
The sweater that's too tight?

What is it about homework
That makes me pick up socks
That stink from days and days of wear,
Then clean the litter box?

What is it about homework
That makes me volunteer
To take the garbage out before
The bugs and flies appear?

What is it about homework
That makes me wash my hair
And take an hour combing out
The snags and tangles there?

What is it about homework?
You know, I wish I knew,
'Cause nights when I've got homework
I've got much too much to do!

Jane Yolen

55

Country School

The Apple Valley School has closed its books,
wiped off its blackboard, put away its chalk;
the valley children with their parents' looks
ride buses down the road their parents walked.

The Apple Valley School is full of bales,
and the bell was auctioned off a year ago.
Under the teeter-totter, spotted quail
have nested where the grass would never grow.

The well is dry where boys caught garter snakes
and chased the girls into their memories.
High on the hill, nobody climbs to shake
the few ripe apples from the broken tree.

Ted Kooser

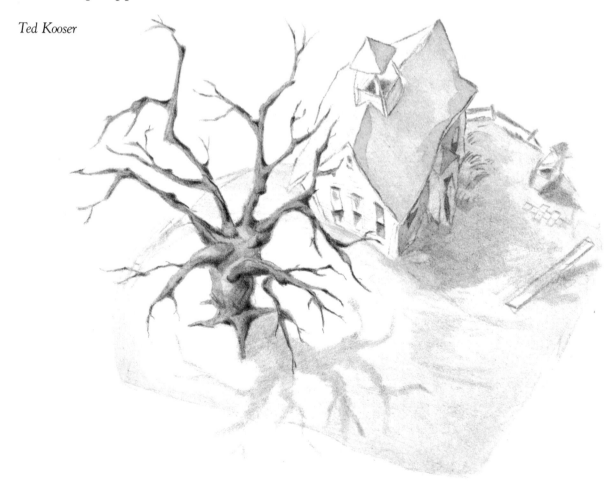

Mystery Story

A morning in May,
And we rolled up to school
In the usual way.

Well no, we didn't really,
Because the school wasn't there;
We rolled up to where
The school *had been*.
There was nothing.
It had all gone
And there wasn't a clue:
No hole, no scar,
Just a buttercup field
And a couple of larks
Singing over it.

You'd have thought there might be
A lot of cheering from the kids,
But there wasn't.
They all just stood around
Wondering,
Not even talking much.

Eric Finney

First Day of Summer

So hushed the pupils at their play
You'd never guess this is the day
When school lets out for the whole summer.

Across the common, even dumber,
Vacationing city folk in pairs
Face newspapers in rocking chairs.

Maybe it's not for me to say —
I am a relative newcomer —
But someone ought to say hurray.

James Hayford

Index of Authors

Index of Titles

Acknowledgments

Arnold Adoff: "Those Who Do Not Study History Are Doomed" and "In This Last Class Before Lunch, I Close My Eyes" from *Chocolate Dreams: Poems by Arnold Adoff*. Text copyright © 1989 by Arnold Adoff. Reprinted by permission of Lothrop, Lee and Shepard Books, a division of William Morrow and Company, Inc.

Edward Anthony: "Duty of the Student" from *Golden Treasury of Poetry*, edited by Louis Untermeyer, reprinted by permission of Mrs. Esther Anthony.

Marchette Chute: "Crayons" and "School Concert" from *Rhymes About Us*, by Marchette Chute. Published 1974 by E. P. Dutton. Copyright © 1974 by Marchette Chute. Reprinted by permission of Elizabeth Roach.

William Cole: "Banananananananana" from *A Boy Named Mary Jane*, by William Cole. Reprinted by permission of the author.

Stanley Cook: "In the Playground" from *Word Houses*, "The Gerbil" from *Come Along*. Reprinted by permission of Mrs. Sarah Matthews.

Robert Currie: "The Schoolbus Comes Before the Sun" from *Yarrow*, by Robert Currie. Reprinted by permission of Oberon Press.

Eleanor Farjeon: "Yawning" from *Eleanor Farjeon's Poems for Children*, by Eleanor Farjeon. Originally appeared in *Sing for Your Supper*, by Eleanor Farjeon. Copyright 1938 by Eleanor Farjeon. Renewed 1966 by Gervase Farjeon. Reprinted by permission of HarperCollins Publishers.

Eric Finney: "Mystery Story" reprinted by permission of the author.

Aileen Fisher: "Back to School," "Wind Circles," and "Difference" from *Out in the Dark and Daylight*, by Aileen Fisher. Text copyright © 1980 by Aileen Fisher. Reprinted by permission of HarperCollins Publishers.

Julia Flores-Morales: "Barrio School" reprinted by permission of the author.

Nikki Giovanni: "education" from *Spin a Soft Black Song*, by Nikki Giovanni. Copyright © 1971, 1985 by Nikki Giovanni. Reprinted by permission of Farrar, Straus & Giroux, Inc.

Nikki Grimes: "I don't understand" from *Something On My Mind*, by Nikki Grimes. Copyright © 1978 by Nikki Grimes. Used by permission of Dial Books for Young Readers, a division of Penguin Books USA Inc.

Katy Hall: "Lunch" from *Breakfast, Books & Dreams: A Day in Verse*, edited by Michael Patrick Hearn. Copyright © 1981 by Katy Hall. Reprinted by permission of the author and Ellen Levine Literary Agency, Inc.

James Hayford: "First Day of Summer" from *Star in the Shed Window: Collected Poems 1933–1988*, by James Hayford. Copyright © 1989 by James Hayford. Reprinted with the permission of The New England Press, Inc., Shelburne, VT.

Russell Hoban: "School Buses" from *The Pedaling Man and Other Poems*, by Russell Hoban. Copyright © 1968 by Russell Hoban. Reprinted by permission of Aitken, Stone & Wylie. "Homework" from *Egg Thoughts and Other Frances Songs*, by Russell Hoban. Text copyright © 1964, 1972 by Russell Hoban. Reprinted by permission of HarperCollins Publishers.

Patricia Hubbell: "Equations" reprinted with permission of Atheneum Publishers, an imprint of Macmillan Publishing Company, from *Catch Me a Wind*, by Patricia Hubbell. Copyright © 1968 by Patricia Hubbell.

Bobbi Katz: "Remembering: The First Day of School" copyright © 1974 by Bobbi Katz. Used by permission of the author, who controls all rights.

X. J. Kennedy: "Teacher" and "Art Class" reprinted with permission of Margaret K. McElderry Books, an imprint of Macmillan Publishing Company, from *The Forgetful Wishing Well*, by X. J. Kennedy. Copyright © 1985 by X. J. Kennedy. "Science Lesson" reprinted by permission of the author. "Mixed-Up School" from *One Winter Night in August*, by X. J. Kennedy. Copyright © 1975 by X. J. Kennedy. Reprinted by permission of Curtis Brown Ltd.

Ted Kooser: "Country School" from *Official Entry Blank: Poems by Ted Kooser*, reprinted by permission of the author.

Karla Kuskin: "Going to School" from *Breakfast, Books & Dreams*, edited by Michael Patrick Hearn. Reprinted by permission of the author.